First Guide to Government

What's the Constitution?

Revised Edition

Nancy Harris

capstone

an imprint of Capstone Global Library, LLC. Chicago, Illinois

To contact Capstone Global Library, please
call 800-747-4992, or visit our web site
www.capstonepub.com

Editorial: Rebecca Rissman
Design: Kimberly R. Miracle and Betsy Wernert
Illustrations: Mapping Specialists
Photo Research: Tracy Cummins and Heather Mauldin
Production: Duncan Gilbert

Library of Congress Cataloging-in-Publication Data
is available on the Library of Congress website.
ISBN 978-1-4846-3690-9 (revised paperback)
ISBN 978-1-4846-3497-4 (ebook)

Photo Credits

Alamy: Glow Images, 5; Capstone Press: Mapping Specialists, 8, 15, 20; Corbis: Bettmann/Joe Marquette, 22, Ken Cedeno, 6; Dreamstime: Americanspirit, 16; Jupiter Images: Tetra Images, Cover; Library of Congress: 9, 11, 13 (all); National Archives and Records Administration: 4, 23, 25, 28; Newscom: Picture History, 12, ROGER L. WOLLENBERG/UPI Photo Service, 29; Shutterstock: Bob Ainsworth, 24, Everett Historical, 10, 27, Mike Flippo, 17, Ricardo Garza, 21; Thinkstock: John Moore, 7; Wikimedia: 14, Steve Petteway, Collection of the Supreme Court of the United States, 19

The publishers would like to thank Nancy Harris for her assistance in the preparation of this book.

Printed in the United States 5242

Table of Contents

Some words are shown in bold, **like this**. You can find out what they mean by looking in the glossary.

What Is the United States Constitution?

The United States Constitution is a very important **document** (paper). It was written by a group of men who lived in the United States of America. At the time when the Constitution was written, the United States was a new country.

We the People

Article. I

Article. II

Article. III

Article. IV

Article. V

Article. VI

Article. VII

done

The Constitution is four pages long.

★ The capitol of the United States is in Washingon, D.C.

The Constitution was written to explain how the United States **federal government** should work. The federal government leads the entire country. The Constitution is a written **law** (rule) that the federal government must follow.

★ The Constitution gives people the freedom of speech.

The Constitution describes the **rights** of people in the United States. Rights are freedoms that people have. These rights include the right to say what you believe. The **law** of the Constitution must be followed by everyone in the United States.

★ The Constitution gives new citizens rights.

The Constitution can be changed. These changes are called **amendments**. Amendments are made to meet the needs of the country or individual states. They are made to meet the needs of **citizens** in the United States. Citizens are people who live in the United States and can vote for their leaders.

History of the Constitution

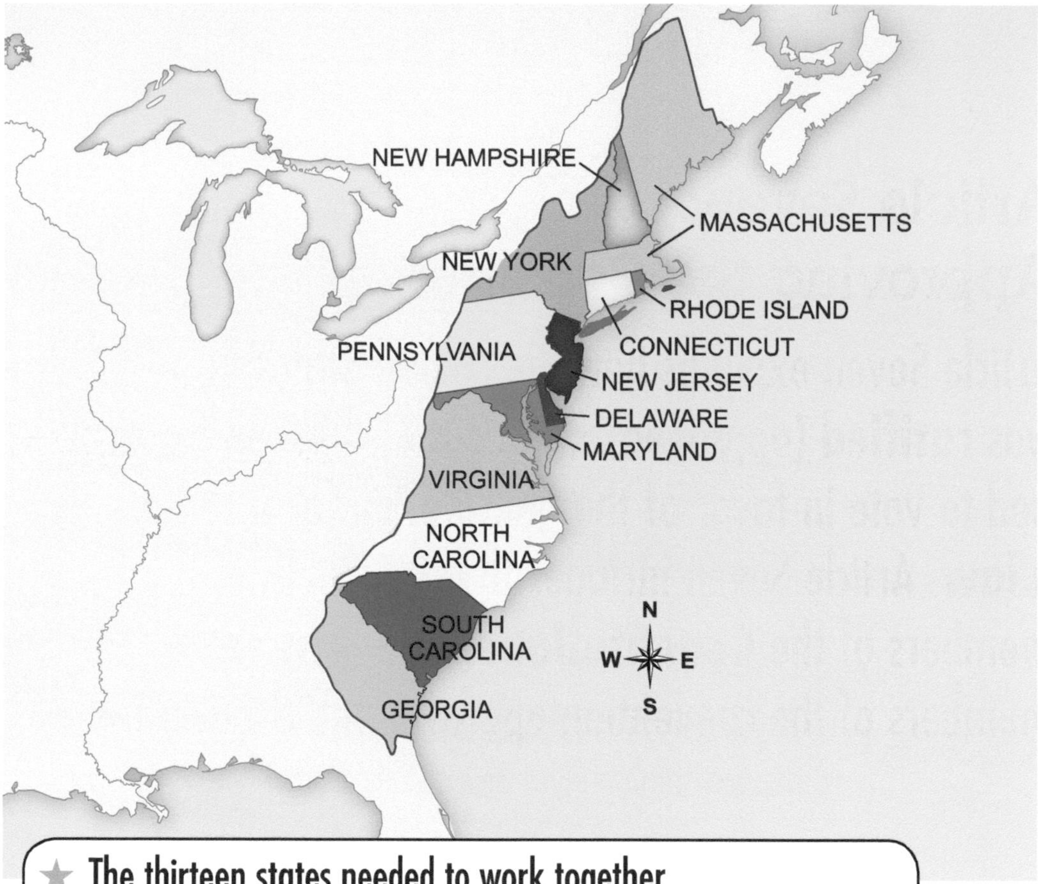

The thirteen states needed to work together.

When the United States of America first became a country, there were only thirteen states. Each state had its own **document** that said how its **state government** would run the state.

In 1776, people in the states joined together to create the United States. They decided they needed a government to lead all the states. They decided to write a document to create rules for how this government would work.

★ Important people met to create the new government.

The Articles of Confederation

The document was called the **Articles of Confederation**. It was written in 1781. The Articles of Confederation did not give the government a lot of power over the states. People realized this was not working.

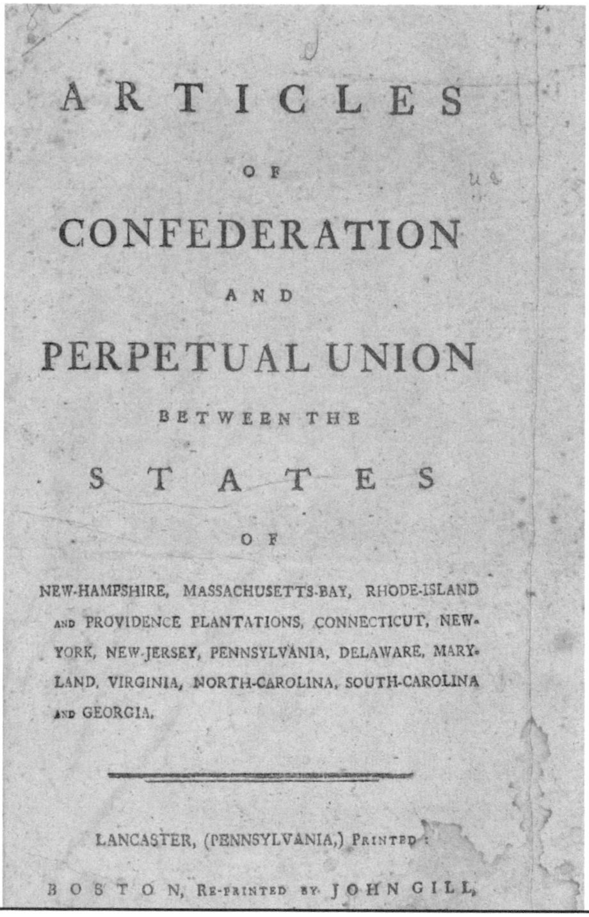

ARTICLES

OF

CONFEDERATION

AND

PERPETUAL UNION

BETWEEN THE

STATES

OF

NEW-HAMPSHIRE, MASSACHUSETTS-BAY, RHODE-ISLAND AND PROVIDENCE PLANTATIONS, CONNECTICUT, NEW-YORK, NEW-JERSEY, PENNSYLVANIA, DELAWARE, MARY-LAND, VIRGINIA, NORTH-CAROLINA, SOUTH-CAROLINA AND GEORGIA.

LANCASTER, (PENNSYLVANIA,) PRINTED:

BOSTON, RE-PRINTED BY JOHN GILL,

★ This is a printed copy of the Articles of Confederation.

The states needed a stronger government to lead them. They decided to rewrite the Articles of Confederation. They held a meeting in the city of Philadelphia. The meeting was called the **Constitutional Convention**.

★ Leaders met at Independence Hall in Philadelphia.

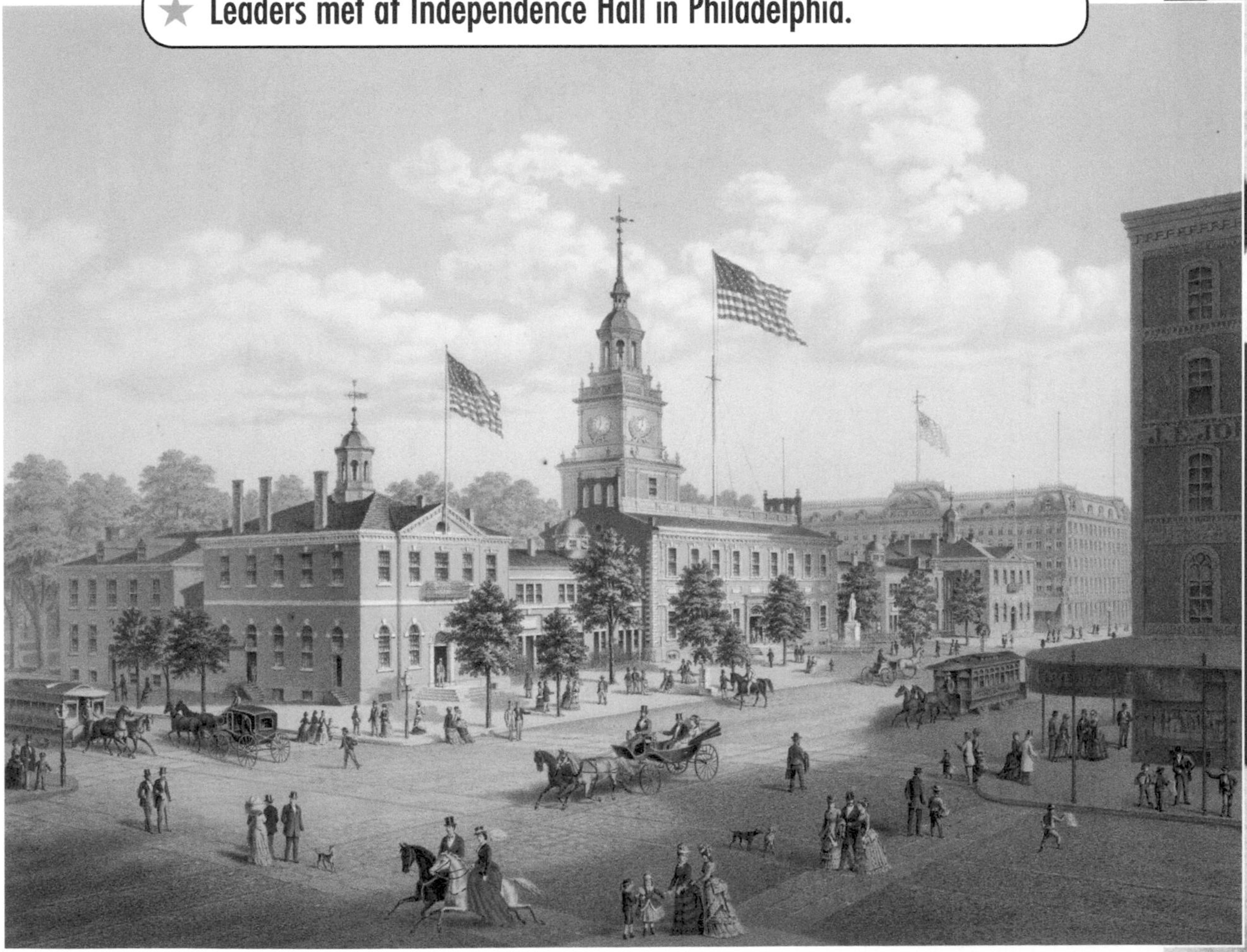

Writing the Constitution

The meeting included a man from each state except the state of Rhode Island. People at the meeting decided that they would write a new **document** called the United States Constitution. This document would replace the **Articles of Confederation**.

State leaders discussed the kind of government they would create.

★ George Washington

★ Benjamin Franklin

★ James Madison

★ Alexander Hamilton

The Constitution was written by a group of men. They decided how the **federal government** would work. Some of these men were James Madison, Alexander Hamilton, George Washington, and Benjamin Franklin.

After the Constitution was approved, it was signed.

The United States Constitution was written in 1787. On September 17, 1787, it was **approved** by the men who attended the **Constitutional Convention**. It also had to be accepted by the states.

In order to become a **law**, nine states had to vote in favor of the Constitution. The state of New Hampshire was the ninth state to approve the Constitution. This happened in June of 1788. The Constitution then replaced the **Articles of Confederation**.

Today there are 50 states. They all must obey the law of the US Constitution.

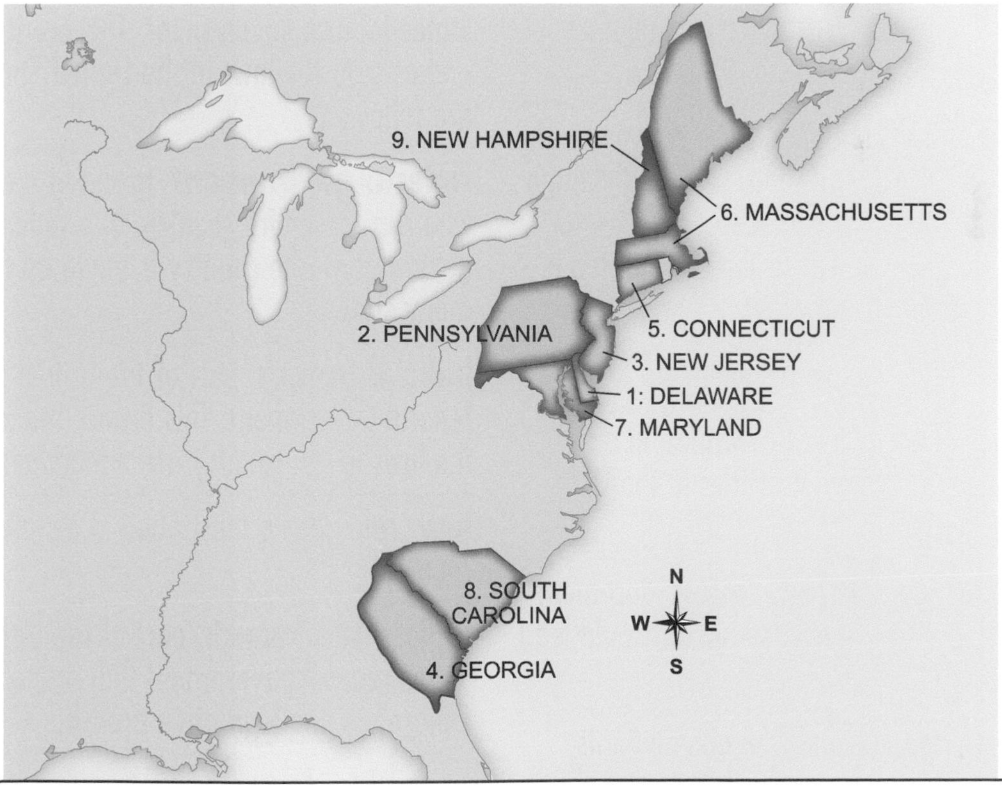

★ These are the first nine states to vote for the Constitution.

Parts of the Constitution

The United States Constitution has three parts:

- the **preamble** (tells why the Constitution was written)
- the **articles** (tells how the federal government works)
- the **amendments** (lists changes to the Constitution)

★ The Constitution is on display in Washington, D.C.

The Preamble

The preamble is the first part of the Constitution. It explains why the Constitution was written. It was written to form a strong **federal** government.

★ The preamble introduces the Constitution.

Articles One, Two, and Three: The Federal Government

There are seven **articles** in the Constitution. The first three articles describe how the **federal government** works. The founding fathers divided the federal government into three branches (parts). These are:

- The **legislative branch** (Article One)
- The **executive branch** (Article Two)
- The **judicial branch** (Article Three)

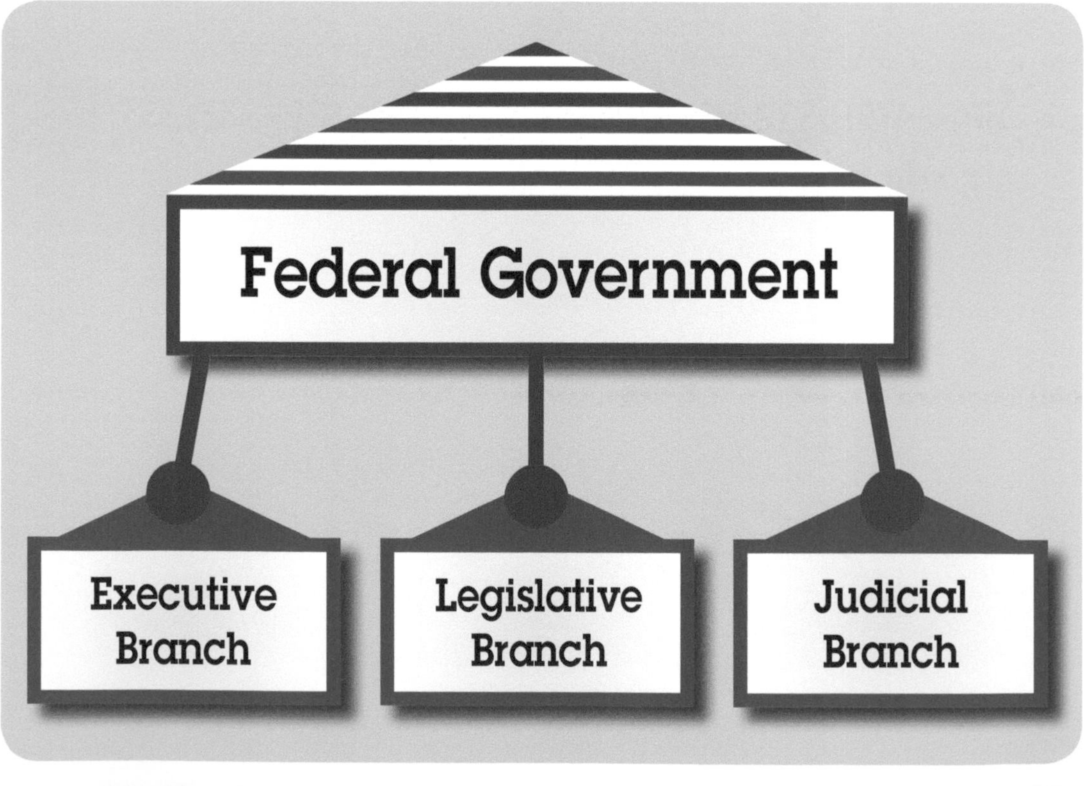

★ These are the Supreme Court Judges.

The first three articles describe the job of each branch of the government. The legislative branch makes laws for the country. The executive branch makes sure the laws are followed. The judicial branch decides if a law has been broken.

Each part of the federal government meets in Washington, D.C.

The first three **articles** explain how the three branches must work together. The branches have different jobs, but they must agree with the decisions of the other two branches. One branch cannot make decisions for the entire country.

Article Four: State Governments

Article Four describes how the **state governments** work with the **federal government**. It also describes how states work with each other. Article Four says that each state can make its own **laws**. States must also follow federal laws.

★ Each state has its own government.

Article Five: Changing the Constitution

The 27th Amendment was the last amendment added to the Constitution.

The Constitution can be **amended** (changed). Article Five describes how to amend the Constitution. It takes a long time to add a new **amendment** to the Constitution. People in the **federal government** and the states must vote in favor of the amendment for it to be added.

Congress may by general Laws prescribe the Manner in which such Acts, Records and Proceedings shall be proved, and the Effect thereof.

Section. 2. The Citizens of each State shall be entitled to all Privileges and Immunities of Citizens in the several States.

A Person charged in any State with Treason, Felony, or other Crime, who shall flee from Justice, and be found in another State, shall on Demand of the executive Authority of the State from which he fled, be delivered up, to be removed to the State having Jurisdiction of the Crime.

No Person held to Service or Labour in one State, under the Laws thereof, escaping into another, shall, in Consequence of any Law or Regulation therein, be discharged from such Service or Labour, but shall be delivered up on Claim of the Party to whom such Service or Labour may be due.

Section. 3. New States may be admitted by the Congress into this Union; but no new State shall be formed or erected within the Jurisdiction of any other State; nor any State be formed by the Junction of two or more States, or Parts of States, without the Consent of the Legislatures of the States concerned as well as of the Congress.

on Application of the Legislature, or of the Executive (when the Legislature cannot be convened) against domestic Violence.

Article. V.

The Congress, whenever two thirds of both Houses shall deem it necessary, shall propose Amendments to this Constitution, or, on the Application of the Legislatures of two thirds of the several States, shall call a Convention for proposing Amendments, which, in either Case, shall be valid to all Intents and Purposes, as Part of this Constitution, when ratified by the Legislatures of three fourths of the several States, or by Conventions in three fourths thereof, as the one or the other Mode of Ratification may be proposed by the Congress; Provided that no Amendment which may be made prior to the Year One thousand eight hundred and eight shall in any Manner affect the first and fourth Clauses in the Ninth Section of the first Article; and that no State, without its Consent, shall be deprived of its equal Suffrage in the Senate.

Article. VI.

All Debts contracted and Engagements entered into, before the Adoption of this Constitution, shall be as valid against the United States under this Constitution, as under the Confederation.

This Constitution, and the Laws of the United States which shall be made in Pursuance thereof; and all Treaties made, or which shall be made, under the Authority of the United States, shall be the supreme Law of the Land; and the Judges in every State shall be bound thereby, any Thing in the Constitution or Laws of any State to the Contrary notwithstanding.

The Senators and Representatives before mentioned, and the Members of the several State Legislatures, and all executive and judicial Officers, both of the United States and of the several States, shall be bound by Oath or Affirmation, to support this Constitution; but no religious Test shall ever be required as a Qualification to any Office or public Trust under the United States.

Article. VII.

The Ratification of the Conventions of nine States, shall be sufficient for the Establishment of this Constitution between the States so ratifying the Same.

done in Convention by the Unanimous Consent of the States present the Seventeenth Day of September in the Year of our Lord one thousand seven hundred and Eighty seven and of the Independance of the United States of America the Twelfth In witness whereof We have hereunto subscribed our Names,

Attest William Jackson Secretary

Go. Washington — Presidt. and deputy from Virginia

Delaware — Geo: Read, Gunning Bedford jun, John Dickinson

New Hampshire — John Langdon, Nicholas Gilman

Maryland

Article Five helps the government meet the needs of its people.

Article Five makes the Constitution a special document. It allows the Constitution to change when the needs of American **citizens** change. The Constitution can be amended at any time.

Article Six: Paying Debts

Article Six says that the **federal government** will pay money it owes to other people or countries. This article was written because the founding fathers wanted to be sure to pay any debts owed by the new country.

The Constitution tells Americans that the United States will repay its debts.

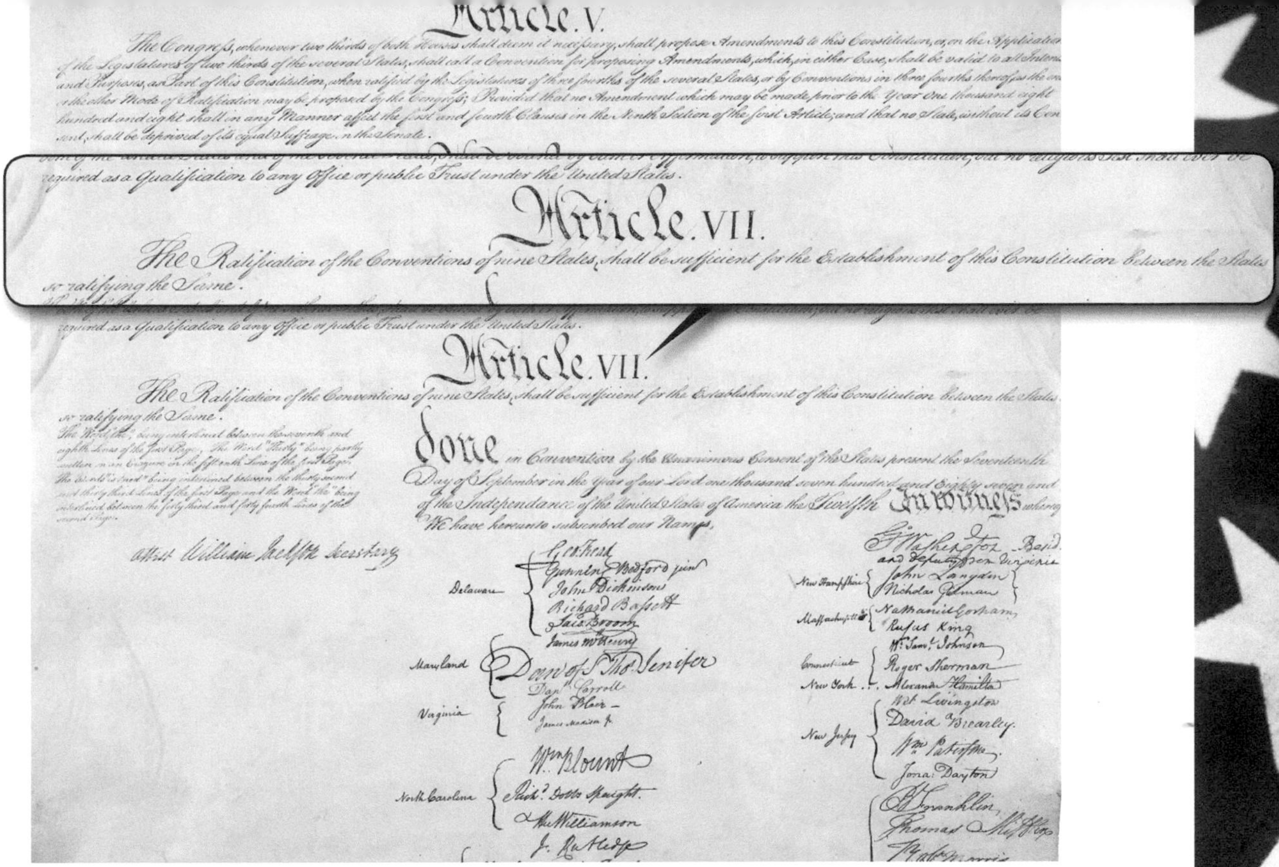

Article Seven: Approving the Constitution

Article Seven explains how the United States Constitution was **ratified** (approved). Nine out of thirteen states had to vote in favor of the Constitution for it to become a **law**. Article Seven includes the signatures of the members of the **Constitutional Convention**. All the members of the convention approved the document.

The Amendments

The last part of the United States Constitution is the **amendments**. These are changes that have been made to the Constitution. These changes are new **laws** that are added to the Constitution.

The first ten amendments were ratified (approved) on December 15, 1791. They are called the **Bill of Rights**. These ten laws protect people's rights or freedoms. They were added just four years after the Constitution had been written.

Congress of the United States,
begun and held at the City of New-York, on
Wednesday the fourth of March, one thousand seven hundred and eighty nine.

THE

RESOLVED

ARTICLES

Article the first.

Article the second.

Article the third.

Article the fourth. A well regulated Militia, being necessary to the security of a free State, the right of the people to keep and bear Arms, shall not be infringed.

Article the fifth.

Article the sixth.

Article the seventh.

Article the eighth.

Article the ninth.

Article the tenth.

Article the eleventh.

Article the twelfth.

Attest,

Speaker of the House of Representatives.

John Adams, Vice President of the United States, and President of the Senate.

Ten of the first twelve amendments were approved and became the Bill of Rights.

Why Is the Constitution Important?

The United States Constitution is the highest **law** in the United States. The Constitution created the **federal government**.

We the People of the United States, in Order to form a more perfect Union, establish Justice, insure domestic Tranquility, provide for the common defence, promote the general Welfare, and secure the Blessings of Liberty to ourselves and our Posterity, do ordain and establish this Constitution for the United States of America.

Article. I.

Section. 1. All legislative Powers herein granted shall be vested in a Congress of the United States, which shall consist of a Senate and House of Representatives.

The Constitution gave people in the United States rights and freedoms.

The Constitution states the rights of people living in the United States. It is written to protect the rights of people living in the United States.

★ You can see the Constitution in Washington, D.C.

Glossary

amend change a piece of text. You can amend the Constitution by adding a new law.

amendment change made to a piece of writing. The change could be a text change or something that has been added to the text. An amendment to the Constitution is when you add a new law.

approve agree with something

article part or piece of writing in a text. There are seven articles in the US Constitution.

Articles of Confederation document that stated how the government would lead all the states.

Bill of Rights first ten amendments. These changes were added to protect the rights (freedoms) of people who live in the United States.

citizen person who is born in the United States. People who have moved to the United States from another country can become citizens by taking a test.

Constitutional Convention meeting held in the city of Philadelphia. The men at this meeting decided to write the US constitution.

document written text or paper. The US Constitution is a document.

executive branch part of the United States federal government. This branch makes sure the laws in the United States are followed.

federal government group of leaders who run the entire country. In a federal government, the country is made up of many states.

judicial branch part of the United States federal government. This branch makes sure the laws in the country are understood.

law rule people must obey in a state or country

legislative branch part of the United States federal government that makes laws. Congress is the legislative branch.

preamble first part of a text. It is written to tell why the paper was written.

ratify agree with something

rights freedoms that people have. Rights include the right to say and write what you think.

state government group of leaders who run a state. Each state in the United States has a state government.

Find Out More

Books to Read

An older reader can help you with these books:

Levy, Elizabeth. *If You Were There When They Signed the Constitution.* New York: Scholastic, 2006.

Pearl, Norman. *The Bill of Rights.* Mankato, MN: Picture Window Books, 2007.

Teitelbaum, Michael. *The U.S. Constitution.* Mankato, MN: Child's World, 2005.

Internet Sites

FactHound offers a safe, fun way to find Internet sites related to this book. All of the sites on FactHound have been researched by our staff

Visit www.fachound.com

Viewing the US Constitution

The US Constitution is on display in the National Archives in the Rotunda. The rotunda is open daily from 9 am to 5 pm.

The National Archives address is:
700 Pennsylvania Avenue, NW
Washington, DC 20408

Index